I0017230

RAG Models Decoded

From Theory to Practice in Retrieval-Augmented Generation

Vijay Bhoyar

© 2024 by Vijay V. Bhoyar

All rights reserved. No part of this publication may be reproduced, distributed, or transmitted in any form or by any means, including photocopying, recording, or other electronic or mechanical methods, without the prior written permission of the publisher, except in the case of brief quotations embodied in critical reviews and certain other noncommercial uses permitted by copyright law. For permission requests, write to the publisher.

Self Publish
First Edition: Mar 2024
Second Edition: July 2025

ISBN: 9798321652053

Names: Vijay V. Bhoyar.
Title: RAG Models Decoded: From Theory to Practice in Retrieval-Augmented Generation

Description: First Edition.

This book is designed to provide a comprehensive understanding of Retrieval-Augmented Generation (RAG) models within the field of natural language processing (NLP). It serves as an educational resource that covers both theoretical foundations and practical applications of RAG models. The content is derived from the author's research, experiences in NLP, and contributions from leading experts in the field. While technical in nature, the book aims to be accessible to readers with a keen interest in artificial intelligence and machine learning. The use cases, strategies, and insights are intended for educational and professional development purposes. The author and publisher are not responsible for any specific outcomes or results from the application of the techniques described herein.

Printed in the USA
www.aiamigos.org

July 2025

Vijay Bhoyar

Table of Contents

Acknowledgments

In writing "RAG Models Decoded: From Theory to Practice in Retrieval-Augmented," I've relied on the valuable feedback from many people. I want to express my deep thanks to everyone who offered constructive criticism. Your insights and challenges have significantly shaped this book, making it better in every way. Your contributions have helped make the topic of RAG models clearer and more interesting for everyone. Thank you for your support and guidance throughout this process.

Vijay V Bhoyar

Vijay Bhoyar

Introduction

Decoding the Power and Potential of RAG Models

Language models like GPT-4 have transformed how we interact with machines, but they come with inherent limitations. They can hallucinate facts, rely on outdated training data, and often lack the ability to provide contextually grounded answers. Retrieval-Augmented Generation (RAG) models solve these challenges by merging two powerful capabilities real-time information retrieval and natural language generation. The result? Responses that are not only fluent but also accurate, current, and knowledge-rich.

This book, **RAG Models Decoded: From Theory to Practice in Retrieval-Augmented Generation**, is designed to help you navigate this exciting frontier of AI. Whether you're a developer building intelligent assistants, a data scientist exploring NLP optimization, or a student eager to understand cutting-edge architectures, this guide provides both theory and actionable steps to master RAG.

What You'll Learn in This Book

By the end of this journey, you will:

- **Understand RAG Architecture** – Explore how encoders, retrievers, and decoders work together to integrate external knowledge into generation pipelines.
- **Master RAG Variants** – Dive into Conditional RAG, Self-RAG, Dense RAG, BART-based RAG, and the future of Agentic RAG with practical comparisons.
- **Apply Proven Optimization Techniques** – Learn about vector databases, data chunking, RAFT fine-tuning, and LoRA for building efficient, domain-specific RAG solutions.
- **Explore Real-World Applications** – See how RAG models are transforming industries such as healthcare, finance, legal, and e-commerce.
- **Get Hands-On with Code and Templates** – Use ready-to-deploy Python scripts and templates to implement RAG models quickly.

Why RAG Matters

In an era where knowledge changes rapidly, static models fall short. RAG represents the next generation of AI models that can dynamically fetch, verify, and synthesize information, bridging the gap between large language models and reliable, real-world data. With this book, you'll gain the tools, techniques, and insights to build AI systems that are both intelligent and trustworthy.

Vijay Bhoyar

Chapter 1

From Traditional NLP to Retrieval-Augmented Generation

1.1 A Brief Evolution of Natural Language Processing (NLP)

Natural Language Processing (NLP) – the science of teaching machines to understand and generate human language – has evolved dramatically over the past few decades.

- **Rule-Based Systems:** Early NLP relied on hand-crafted rules, which were rigid and failed to scale with real-world language complexity.
- **Statistical NLP:** In the 2000s, statistical methods like n-grams and Hidden Markov Models improved tasks such as machine translation but lacked deep semantic understanding.
- **Neural Networks and Transformers:** The past decade ushered in deep learning and Transformer-based models (e.g., BERT, GPT), enabling significant breakthroughs in text classification, summarization, and creative text generation.

Despite these advances, **traditional text generation models** still face key limitations. Understanding these shortcomings helps explain why Retrieval-Augmented Generation (RAG) emerged as the next logical step in NLP.

1.2 Challenges of Traditional Text Generation Models

Even large Transformer-based models like GPT-3 or T5, powerful as they are, suffer from three major challenges:

1. **Constrained Knowledge Base**
   These models can only generate answers based on the data they were trained on. If the training data is outdated or incomplete, outputs can be factually incorrect or misleading.
   Example: A model trained on a 2020 dataset may not know about scientific breakthroughs from 2023.
2. **Limited Contextual Understanding**
   Traditional models often fail to fully grasp the nuance of a user's query or adapt to specific contexts.
   Example: A model trained on legal documents might generate generic legal advice, missing the personalized guidance needed for a real consultation.

3. **Repetitiveness and Lack of Creativity**
   Generative models tend to recycle phrases or produce content that feels formulaic.
   Example A recipe-generation model might produce nearly identical cooking instructions, even for vastly different cuisines.

These weaknesses highlight the need for a smarter, context-aware generation system – one that can supplement its learned patterns with *real-time, relevant knowledge retrieval.*

1.3 The Emergence of Retrieval-Augmented Generation (RAG)

Retrieval-Augmented Generation is a powerful approach that integrates two capabilities:

1. **Retrieval:** Actively fetching relevant information from an external knowledge base, database, or document collection.
2. **Generation:** Using a language model (like BART or T5) to synthesize a coherent, contextually relevant response from both the user prompt and retrieved data.

This combination allows RAG models to:

- **Overcome Knowledge Gaps:** By querying up-to-date sources, RAG models can produce accurate, current answers.
- **Deepen Context Awareness:** The integration of retrieved content ensures responses are not just fluent but also grounded in the right context.
- **Encourage Freshness and Diversity:** By drawing on a wide range of sources, RAG models can generate responses that are more creative and less repetitive.

Example:
If asked, *"What is quantum computing?"*, a RAG model will first retrieve a relevant article or research snippet, then generate a concise, well-informed answer that blends the retrieved content with natural language fluency.

1.4 Why RAG Matters

RAG represents a paradigm shift in NLP. Rather than relying solely on what the model *memorized*, RAG connects generation with dynamic knowledge retrieval, enabling:

- More accurate Q&A systems.
- Domain-specific chatbots (e.g., medical or financial).
- Search-assisted content creation.

As this book unfolds, we will explore the core architecture of RAG (encoder, retriever, decoder), its variants (e.g., Conditional RAG, Self-RAG), and how these models are applied across industries. This journey begins with a deep understanding of the foundational components, which we explore next in Chapter.

Key Takeaways from Chapter 1

Traditional NLP models, even Transformers, have knowledge and context limitations.

RAG combines retrieval with generation to produce more accurate and contextually rich responses.

RAG is not just an evolution of NLP but a bridge between static language models and dynamic, knowledge-aware AI systems.

Chapter 2

Demystifying RAG Models: Core Concepts and Advantages

2.1 What Makes RAG Different?

Traditional generative models like GPT or T5 produce text based solely on their training data. While they excel at fluency, they often hallucinate facts or fail to incorporate the latest knowledge. Retrieval-Augmented Generation (RAG) solves these problems by introducing an additional step: retrieval of real-world information.

Instead of relying only on memorized patterns, a RAG model dynamically searches external knowledge sources like databases, document collections, or the web and then generates a response that combines the retrieved content with the user query. This makes the output more accurate, up-to-date, and context-aware.

Key Advantage:
A RAG model behaves like a well-informed expert. It doesn't just recall what it knows it researches on the fly, then synthesizes an answer tailored to your question.

2.2 The Core Architecture: Encoder, Retriever, and Decoder

Think of RAG as a team of three collaborators each with a specific role:

1. **Encoder – The Interpreter**
   The encoder (often a Transformer like BERT or RoBERTa) converts the user's query into a semantic vector. This vector captures the *meaning* of the query, much like a skilled interpreter translating a question into the right "language" for retrieval.
2. **Retriever – The Researcher**
   The retriever searches external knowledge bases using the encoded query.
   o It might use vector similarity search to find documents with the closest meaning to the query.
   o Tools like FAISS, Milvus, or Pinecone often power this retrieval step.
   The retriever ensures the model has the right facts before generation begins.
3. **Decoder – The Storyteller**
   The decoder (e.g., BART, T5, or GPT) takes the original query plus the

retrieved documents and crafts a final, coherent response. It merges the factual content from retrieval with natural language fluency.

Why It Works:
The encoder ensures the right "question" is asked, the retriever supplies the best answers, and the decoder weaves everything into human-like text. Together, they create responses that are accurate, context-rich, and readable.

2.3 Retrieval Mechanisms Explained

Not all retrieval strategies are created equal. RAG systems use various methods to find relevant information:

- **Keyword Matching (Basic Search):**
  Similar to a search engine that matches words, this method is fast but may miss context if the phrasing differs.
- **Vector-Based Semantic Search:**
  Both queries and documents are transformed into high-dimensional vectors. The retriever finds documents with **similar meaning** even if they don't share the same words. This is the default method in modern RAG systems.
- **Advanced Neural Retrieval:**
  Some RAG models use fine-tuned deep learning retrievers (like Dense Passage Retrieval, DPR) to ensure contextual accuracy and relevance.

2.4 Example Walkthrough: How RAG Answers a Question

Query: "What is quantum computing?"

1. **Encoding:**
   The encoder transforms this question into a dense vector representing its meaning.
2. **Retrieval:**
   The retriever searches a knowledge base (e.g., Wikipedia) for relevant documents, such as:
   - "Quantum computing uses quantum bits (qubits)…"
   - "Unlike classical computing, quantum systems use superposition…"

3. Generation:
The decoder reads the question and the retrieved documents, then generates a response:
"Quantum computing is a type of computing that uses quantum bits (qubits) to perform calculations, leveraging principles like superposition and entanglement to solve problems classical computers find difficult."

This three-step pipeline ensures that the answer is not only fluent but factually grounded.

2.5 Why RAG Outperforms Traditional Models

- **Accuracy and Trustworthiness:** RAG can access the latest information, reducing hallucinations and errors.
- **Adaptability:** By swapping or updating the knowledge base, you can tailor RAG to domains like healthcare, finance, or law without retraining the entire model.
- **Efficiency:** Instead of increasing model size (which is costly), RAG enhances capability by combining a smaller model with smarter retrieval.

Key Takeaways from Chapter 2

RAG's power comes from combining retrieval (fact-finding) with generation (natural language creation).

The architecture Encoder, Retriever, Decoder is the backbone of all RAG systems.

With the right retrieval strategy, RAG models are more accurate, customizable, and resource-efficient than traditional large language models.

Chapter 3

Conditional and Self-RAG Models: Tailoring Generation with Context

3.1 Why Variants of RAG?

While the basic RAG framework (Encoder → Retriever → Decoder) is powerful, many tasks require customized retrieval strategies or long-term reasoning. Two prominent RAG variants Conditional RAG (C-RAG) and Self-RAG address these needs by extending RAG's capabilities for context-specific and memory-driven generation.

3.2 Conditional RAG (C-RAG): Adding Contextual Intelligence

What It Is:
Conditional RAG enhances the retrieval process by conditioning searches on additional context such as user preferences, task type, or historical interactions.

How It Works:

- Instead of retrieving documents solely based on the current query, C-RAG injects contextual metadata (e.g., conversation history, domain-specific constraints, or user profiles) into the retrieval step.
- This ensures results are highly targeted and task-specific.

Example Use Case:
Imagine a user asking:

"Tell me about the fastest birds."
A generic RAG model may retrieve technical details about bird flight speeds. A C-RAG system, when conditioned for a children's story, will retrieve kid-friendly facts, such as playful anecdotes about the peregrine falcon, resulting in a context-appropriate narrative.

Benefits of C-RAG:

- Greater relevance due to tailored retrieval.
- Useful for personalized recommendations, chatbots, and domain-specific assistants (e.g., healthcare Q&A).
- Reduces irrelevant or overly generic answers.

3.3 Self-RAG: When Models Build Their Own Memory

What It Is:
Self-RAG enables a model to store and reuse its previous outputs as an internal knowledge base, creating a form of long-term memory.

How It Works:

- As the model generates responses over time, key summaries or outputs are stored in an internal vector database.
- When answering new queries, the model retrieves not only external knowledge but also its own historical answers, ensuring consistency and depth.

Example Use Case:
Consider a research assistant bot summarizing scientific papers over weeks. With Self-RAG, it can consult its own summaries of past papers to answer cross-topic questions (e.g., "Compare quantum computing and bioinformatics approaches to problem-solving").

Benefits of Self-RAG:

- Builds incremental expertise over time.
- Increases consistency across conversations or documents.
- Reduces dependency on constant external calls when information has already been processed.

Challenges:

- Requires quality control stale or incorrect outputs can pollute the internal memory.
- Needs efficient storage and retrieval mechanisms to prevent information overload.

3.4 Multi-Hop Retrieval and Reasoning

Modern RAG research is moving toward multi-hop retrieval, where models:

- Retrieve documents step by step, chaining queries to gather complex, multi-faceted answers.
- Combine multiple retrieval passes with reasoning steps, similar to how a human researcher digs deeper into a topic.

Example:
To answer, *"How has quantum computing influenced modern cryptography?"*, a multi-hop RAG system might:

1. Retrieve information on quantum computing basics.
2. Retrieve papers on quantum cryptography.
3. Combine both contexts to generate a coherent, insight-rich answer.

3.5 Conditional RAG vs. Self-RAG

FEATURE	CONDITIONAL RAG	SELF-RAG
FOCUS	Context-specific retrieval	Long-term internal memory
DATA SOURCE	External knowledge + context filters	External + self-generated knowledge
BEST USE CASES	Personalized chatbots, domain tasks	Research assistants, long-term agents
LIMITATIONS	Requires well-defined context rules	Requires careful quality monitoring

---

Key Takeaways from Chapter 3

C-RAG adapts retrieval based on the context of the task or user, making results more relevant.

Self-RAG allows a model to build its own evolving knowledge base, improving consistency over time.

The future of RAG involves multi-hop reasoning and agentic approaches that combine planning, retrieval, and generation for complex tasks.

C-RAG Architecture

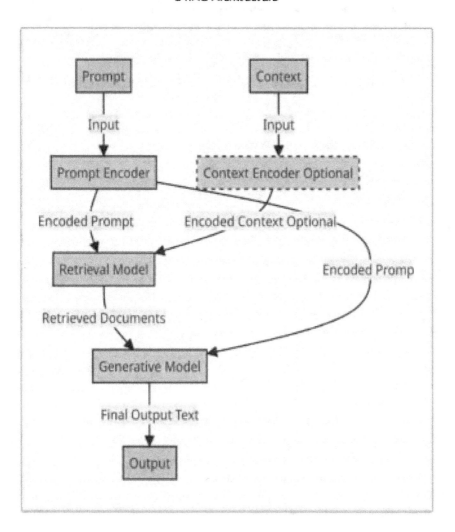

Self-RAG Architecture

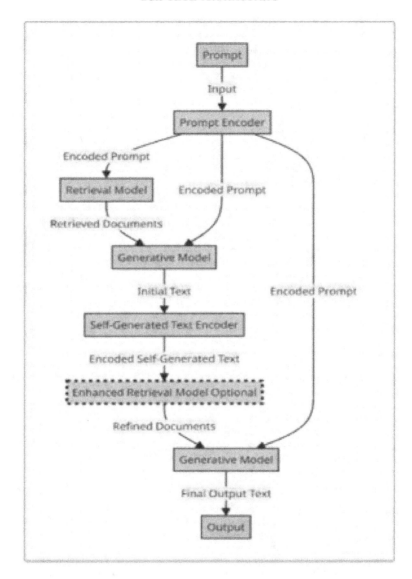

3.6 Agentic RAG: RAG Meets Autonomous Agents

The next evolution of RAG is Agentic RAG, which combines retrieval-augmented generation with the planning and reasoning capabilities of autonomous agents. Instead of simply retrieving and generating a single response, Agentic RAG follows a multi-step reasoning loop retrieving data, analyzing results, and iteratively refining the response until the task is completed.

How Agentic RAG Works

1. **Planning:** The agent first breaks a complex task into smaller steps.

2. **Retrieval + Reasoning Loop:**

    o   At each step, the agent retrieves information, evaluates it, and decides the next action (e.g., retrieve more data, call a tool, or generate partial output).

    o   This loop continues until the agent gathers all necessary context.

3. **Synthesis:** The agent combines all retrieved insights and produces a final, coherent response.

Example: Agentic RAG in Action

Query: *"Create a timeline of major quantum computing breakthroughs and explain their impact on cryptography."*

An Agentic RAG system might:

1. Retrieve documents about quantum computing breakthroughs.
2. Retrieve papers about quantum cryptography.
3. Reason through the connections between the two topics.
4. Generate a detailed timeline and analysis, possibly citing key papers or calling an external API to verify dates.

Key Features of Agentic RAG

*   **Multi-Hop Reasoning:** Chains multiple retrievals to answer multi-faceted queries.

*   **Tool Integration:** Can call APIs, run code snippets, or query structured data alongside unstructured retrieval.

*   **Dynamic Decision-Making:** Uses reasoning (e.g., ReAct framework or chain-of-thought methods) to decide what to retrieve next.

Real-World Applications

- **Research Assistants:** Performing deep, iterative research tasks by combining multiple knowledge sources.

- **Business Intelligence:** Analyzing market trends by pulling data from structured and unstructured databases.

- **Autonomous Chatbots:** Providing multi-step, verifiable answers for customer service or legal queries.

Advantages of Agentic RAG

- **High Accuracy:** Continuous retrieval reduces hallucinations and errors.

- **Complex Task Handling:** Ideal for multi-step reasoning, such as investigative or analytical tasks.

- **Extensibility:** Easily integrates with external tools like search engines, code interpreters, or calculators.

Challenges and Considerations

- **Latency:** Multiple retrieval and reasoning steps increase response time.

- **Cost:** More retrieval and computation mean higher resource consumption.

- **Evaluation Complexity:** Measuring the success of multi-step reasoning requires more robust benchmarks.

Key Takeaway

Agentic RAG represents the future of RAG systems moving from static, one-shot responses to autonomous, reasoning-driven solutions that actively plan, retrieve, and generate knowledge like a human researcher.

Chapter 4

Beyond the Basics: Exploring Advanced RAG Variants

While the foundational RAG architecture (Encoder → Retriever → Decoder) provides a strong baseline, specialized advanced variants have emerged to tackle unique challenges and push the boundaries of performance. These variants are designed to improve retrieval precision, enhance response quality, and even introduce reasoning and planning into the RAG pipeline. In this chapter, we explore **Dense RAG**, **BART-based RAG**, and the cutting-edge **Agentic RAG** paradigm.

4.1 Dense RAG: Elevating Retrieval Precision

What It Is:
Dense RAG replaces simple keyword or sparse retrieval with dense vector representations that capture semantic meaning. Instead of matching documents based on word overlap, Dense RAG leverages neural embeddings to find contextually similar documents.

How It Works:

- Uses **Dense Passage Retrieval (DPR)** or bi-encoder architectures to map both queries and documents into the same vector space.
- Employs vector similarity search (e.g., FAISS, Milvus, Pinecone) to retrieve documents that are conceptually relevant, even if wording differs.

Example:
For the query *"fastest animal on Earth"*, a Dense RAG retriever would return *"Peregrine falcon reaches 320 km/h in a dive"*, even if the word "animal" isn't explicitly in the source text.

Benefits of Dense RAG:

- Improved relevance in retrieval results.
- Handles synonyms, paraphrases, and contextual variations better than keyword search.
- Essential for domain-specific RAG (e.g., legal or biomedical text).

4.2 BART-Based RAG: Superior Generation Quality

What It Is:
BART-based RAG integrates BART (Bidirectional and Auto-Regressive Transformers) as its decoder, enhancing the coherence, fluency, and style of generated text.

How It Works:

- After retrieval, the BART decoder synthesizes the information into natural, context-rich responses.
- BART excels at complex text generation tasks like summarization, storytelling, and creative content creation.

Example:
A standard RAG might produce a bland summary of a news article, while a BART-based RAG could generate a concise, engaging narrative with improved readability and structure.

Benefits of BART-Based RAG:

- Higher quality outputs, especially for creative or explanatory tasks.
- Strong performance across summarization, question answering, and storytelling.
- Can be fine-tuned for tone and style (e.g., formal vs. conversational).

4.3 Agentic RAG: The Next Frontier

What It Is:
Agentic RAG extends traditional RAG by combining retrieval with autonomous reasoning, planning, and tool use. Rather than stopping after a single retrieval step, Agentic RAG follows an iterative "think-retrieve-act" loop to solve complex queries.

Key Features:

- Multi-Hop Retrieval: Breaks a task into smaller sub-queries and retrieves documents across multiple steps.
- Reasoning-Driven Generation: Uses frameworks like ReAct (Reason + Act) to plan actions, decide when to retrieve, and when to generate.
- Tool Integration: Can call external APIs, run code, or query structured data during the reasoning process.

Example:

For a query like *"Explain how quantum computing impacts cybersecurity, with recent examples,"* an Agentic RAG system might:

1. Retrieve the latest quantum computing breakthroughs.
2. Fetch papers on quantum-safe cryptography.
3. Synthesize findings and generate an answer, citing the most recent research.

Benefits of Agentic RAG:

- Excels at complex, multi-step reasoning tasks.
- Reduces hallucinations by iteratively verifying and expanding retrieved information.
- Ideal for research assistants, investigative chatbots, and data-intensive analysis.

Challenges:

- **Latency & Cost:** Multiple retrieval steps increase computational load.
- **Evaluation:** Measuring reasoning quality requires advanced benchmarks.

4.4 Comparing Advanced RAG Variants

VARIANT	FOCUS	STRENGTHS	BEST USE CASES
DENSE RAG	Retrieval precision	Semantic accuracy, domain adaptability	Legal, scientific, or enterprise search
BART-RAG	Output fluency & quality	Coherent, creative, and narrative responses	Summarization, creative writing
AGENTIC RAG	Reasoning & planning	Multi-step retrieval, tool integration	Research, analytics, autonomous agents

4.5 Why Advanced RAG Variants Matter

These advanced RAG models allow practitioners to tailor solutions to specific needs:

- Use **Dense RAG** when accuracy and recall are paramount.
- Use **BART-RAG** when high-quality natural text is needed.
- Use **Agentic RAG** when solving complex, multi-step tasks requiring reasoning.

Key Takeaways from Chapter 4

Dense RAG improves retrieval with semantic vector search.

BART-based RAG boosts generation quality and fluency.

Agentic RAG introduces autonomous reasoning and multi-step task handling, paving the way for the next generation of AI assistants.

Dense-RAG Architecture

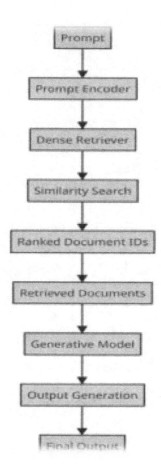

RAG-Transformer Architecture

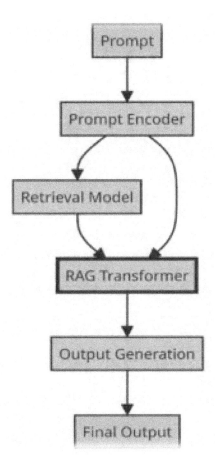

BART-based RAG Architecture

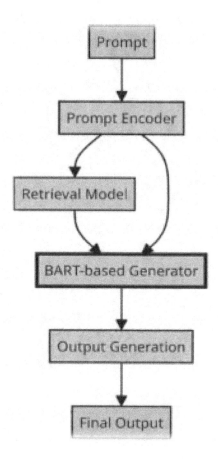

Chapter 5

Agentic RAG: Bridging Retrieval and Autonomy

The landscape of Retrieval-Augmented Generation (RAG) is rapidly evolving. Traditional RAG models follow a straightforward pipeline encode a query, retrieve relevant documents, and generate a response. However, complex tasks such as multi-step reasoning, cross-domain research, or dynamic decision-making require models to go beyond single-pass retrieval. Enter Agentic RAG and other next-generation approaches, which combine retrieval with autonomous agent-like reasoning.

5.1 What Is Agentic RAG?

Agentic RAG transforms the RAG pipeline into a **loop of reasoning and retrieval**, enabling the model to act as an intelligent agent rather than a static text generator. It doesn't stop at retrieving once; instead, it plans a sequence of actions to gather the necessary context, retrieve supporting data, and verify results before finalizing an answer.

Key Characteristics of Agentic RAG:

- **Reasoning Loop:** The model plans *what to retrieve next* based on intermediate results.

- **Tool Use:** It can interact with external tools or APIs for data collection, calculations, or document parsing.

- **Multi-Hop Retrieval:** Chains multiple retrieval queries to gather information from various sources for a comprehensive answer.

5.2 How Agentic RAG Works

1. **Task Decomposition:** The agent breaks a complex query into smaller sub-tasks.

2. **Iterative Retrieval:** Each sub-task triggers a retrieval step, guided by reasoning.

3. **Intermediate Analysis:** The model evaluates retrieved content and decides whether additional retrieval is needed.

4. **Response Synthesis:** Once all relevant data is gathered, the model generates a final, well-structured answer.

5.3 Example Walkthrough

Query: *"Analyze the latest quantum computing breakthroughs and their impact on cybersecurity."*

An Agentic RAG system would:

1. Retrieve and summarize recent quantum computing advancements.

2. Retrieve cybersecurity papers discussing post-quantum cryptography.

3. Connect the two sets of information to explain how quantum computing affects encryption.

4. Optionally call APIs (e.g., arXiv) for the latest publications, ensuring the answer is both current and verified.

5.4 Applications of Agentic RAG

- **Research Assistants:** Iteratively gather and analyze data from multiple domains.

- **Enterprise Analytics:** Correlate reports and KPIs across departments for strategic decision-making.

- **Healthcare:** Combine patient history, medical literature, and clinical guidelines to generate treatment recommendations.

- **Legal Tech:** Conduct multi-step legal research, citing case law and precedents with detailed reasoning.

5.5 Advantages and Challenges

Advantages:

- Handles complex and multi-step tasks better than standard RAG.

- Reduces hallucinations by verifying retrieved content at each step.

- Integrates seamlessly with tools and structured data sources.

Challenges:

- **Higher latency and cost** due to multiple retrieval and reasoning loops.

- **Evaluation complexity:** Harder to benchmark because performance depends on reasoning steps, not just single outputs.

- **Engineering overhead:** Requires orchestration frameworks (e.g., LangChain, ReAct) for agent behavior.

5.6 Next-Generation Trends

Agentic RAG is part of a broader next-generation RAG movement that includes:

- **Multi-hop RAG:** Sequentially retrieves documents for complex question answering.

- **Hybrid RAG:** Combines structured (SQL databases) and unstructured data retrieval.

- **RAG + Tool Use:** Models that can query APIs, run code, or perform calculations alongside retrieval.

Key Takeaway

Agentic RAG represents the shift from static knowledge retrieval to autonomous, reasoning-driven AI systems. It's the next frontier for building intelligent assistants that can plan, reason, and act unlocking new levels of capability for RAG-based solutions.

Agentic RAG

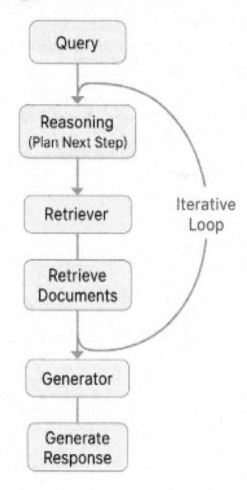

Chapter 6

A Comparative Analysis: Choosing the Right RAG Model

Selecting the right Retrieval-Augmented Generation (RAG) model requires understanding not only the core architecture but also how different variants perform under various conditions. In this chapter, we analyze Dense RAG, BART-based RAG, and Agentic RAG side by side, evaluating them on retrieval performance, generation quality, adaptability, resource requirements, and real-world applicability.

6.1 Criteria for Evaluating RAG Models

When assessing RAG models, several quantitative and qualitative metrics are considered:

1. Retrieval Performance

- **Recall:** Measures the percentage of relevant documents retrieved.
- **NDCG (Normalized Discounted Cumulative Gain):** Evaluates the ranking quality of retrieved documents, prioritizing relevance at the top of the list.

2. Generation Quality

- **BLEU/ROUGE Scores:** Evaluate the overlap between generated text and reference answers for tasks like summarization or question answering.
- **Human Evaluation:** Considers fluency, factual accuracy, and style.

3. Adaptability

- **Domain Transfer:** How well the model performs across different industries or contexts.
- **Customizability:** How easily the model can be fine-tuned for specific tasks.

4. Resource Requirements

- **Compute Cost:** GPU/CPU requirements for retrieval and generation.
- **Latency:** The time required for retrieving and generating responses.

5. Advanced Reasoning Capability

- **Multi-Hop Retrieval:** Ability to perform iterative retrieval for complex, multi-step queries.
- **Tool Integration:** Ability to call APIs, run code, or incorporate structured data.

6.2 Comparative Overview of RAG Variants

FEATURE	DENSE RAG	BART-BASED RAG	AGENTIC RAG
PRIMARY FOCUS	Retrieval precision	High-quality text generation	Multi-step reasoning & autonomy
RETRIEVAL QUALITY	High (semantic dense search)	Moderate (depends on retriever choice)	Very High (iterative multi-hop retrieval)
GENERATION QUALITY	Moderate	Excellent (BART excels at fluency)	High (reasoning + synthesis)
COMPLEX QUERIES	Handles simple queries well	Good for narrative tasks	Best for multi-step, complex reasoning
RESOURCE USAGE	Moderate	Moderate to High	High (due to iterative planning)
BEST USE CASES	Legal, scientific, or enterprise search	Summarization, storytelling, creative Q&A	Research assistants, analytics, autonomous agents

6.3 Choosing the Right RAG Model

1. **For Factual Accuracy and Recall:**
   Choose Dense RAG if the task requires highly relevant document retrieval, such as legal research or biomedical Q&A.
2. **For High-Quality Natural Language Output:**
   BART-Based RAG is ideal when narrative structure, fluency, and style matter, such as generating reports, articles, or customer-facing summaries.
3. **For Complex Analytical Tasks:**
   Agentic RAG shines for multi-step reasoning, iterative search, and scenarios where the model must act like a self-directed researcher.

6.4 Model Selection Framework

To determine which RAG variant fits your needs, consider:

- **Task Complexity:** Do you need single-step answers or reasoning chains?
- **Content Requirements:** Do you prioritize factuality, creativity, or both?
- **Resources:** Can you afford higher compute costs for advanced planning loops?
- **Integration Needs:** Do you require tool calls or structured data access (Agentic RAG)?

6.5 Future Considerations

With advancements like multi-hop retrieval and Agentic RAG, the lines between traditional RAG and autonomous AI agents are blurring. Future models may combine the strengths of Dense, BART-based, and Agentic RAG, offering plug-and-play modules for retrieval, generation, and reasoning.

Key Takeaways from Chapter 6

Dense RAG excels at accuracy and retrieval quality.

BART-Based RAG produces fluent, human-like outputs.

Agentic RAG is the future of RAG, capable of multi-step reasoning and complex decision-making.

Choosing the right RAG model depends on your task goals, domain, and computational resources.

Chapter 7

RAG Models Transforming Industries

Revolutionizing Industries: How RAG Models Are Transforming Businesses

The versatility of Retrieval-Augmented Generation (RAG) models, combined with new advancements like Agentic RAG, is redefining how industries leverage AI for knowledge-intensive tasks. From healthcare to finance, businesses are adopting context-aware, reasoning-driven AI systems to achieve faster decision-making, deeper insights, and improved customer experiences.

7.1 Healthcare: Intelligent Clinical Support

Why RAG Matters in Healthcare:
Medical knowledge evolves rapidly, with thousands of new research papers published daily. Traditional language models often struggle to provide up-to-date, evidence-backed answers, but RAG models excel by retrieving the latest medical studies and combining them with structured patient data.

Key Applications in 2024–2025:

1. **Clinical Decision Support:**
   - Agentic RAG assistants help doctors evaluate treatment options by cross-referencing patient history with the latest medical research and clinical guidelines.
   - Example: A physician asks, *"What's the latest recommended protocol for pediatric asthma management?"* The RAG system retrieves the newest guidelines, synthesizes them with the patient's record, and generates a tailored summary.
2. **Medical Research Assistants:**
   - Agentic RAG models perform multi-step research tasks, retrieving papers from sources like PubMed, extracting key findings, and providing a verified synthesis.
   - These systems can highlight contradictions between studies and even suggest areas for further research.
3. **Patient-Facing Health Chatbots:**
   - RAG-based bots provide personalized health advice, explain lab reports, and link to reliable medical resources.
   - By integrating with electronic health records (EHRs), they deliver context-specific responses while maintaining HIPAA compliance.

7.2 Finance: Risk Analysis and Intelligent Advisory

Why RAG Is a Game-Changer in Finance:
Financial institutions handle vast volumes of unstructured data earnings reports, regulatory updates, and market news. RAG models bridge the gap between real-time data retrieval and high-quality analytical summaries.

Key Applications in 2024–2025:

1. **Agentic Risk Analysis:**
   - An Agentic RAG system can fetch and analyze recent regulatory filings, correlate them with historical market events, and provide a step-by-step risk assessment.
   - For example, when assessing a portfolio, the system iteratively retrieves latest SEC filings, macroeconomic indicators, and generates risk exposure reports.
2. **Personalized Financial Advisory:**
   - RAG-powered advisors can retrieve customer-specific transaction histories, combine them with market trends, and provide tailored investment strategies.
   - Unlike static LLMs, RAG ensures recommendations reflect real-time market data.
3. **Fraud Detection and Compliance Monitoring:**
   - By cross-referencing transaction patterns with regulatory knowledge bases, RAG models can generate alerts for suspicious activity while explaining the reasoning behind flagged transactions.

7.3 Research and Enterprise Knowledge

Why Agentic RAG Excels in Research:
Traditional knowledge management systems cannot perform iterative exploration. Agentic RAG fills this gap with multi-hop retrieval and autonomous reasoning.

Key Applications:

1. **Scientific Discovery:**
   - Agentic RAG tools iterate across multiple disciplines, retrieving papers and generating cross-domain insights.
   - For example, it might connect advancements in quantum computing with cryptography and material science.
2. **Enterprise Knowledge Assistants:**
   - Large organizations can deploy RAG-powered assistants that retrieve information across internal wikis, documents, and ticketing systems helping employees get precise answers faster.
3. **Patent and Legal Research:**

  o Agentic RAG can trace prior patents, analyze legal rulings, and generate summarized insights to assist legal teams.

7.4 Emerging Use Cases for 2025

Beyond healthcare, finance, and research, RAG and Agentic RAG are transforming:

- **E-commerce:** For hyper-personalized product recommendations, combining user history, real-time trends, and product catalogs.
- **Customer Support:** For dynamic, context-aware chatbots that handle multi-turn troubleshooting with accurate retrieval of policies or manuals.
- **Media and Journalism:** For fact-checked content creation, where RAG ensures accuracy by retrieving and citing verified sources.

Key Takeaways from Chapter 7

Healthcare: RAG models are powering clinical decision-making, research synthesis, and patient support.

Finance: Agentic RAG enables real-time risk analysis, compliance, and personalized investment strategies.

Research: Multi-hop retrieval is creating cross-domain insights and accelerating scientific discovery.

The Future: Agentic RAG will drive autonomous, reasoning-driven assistants across industries.

Here's a summary table for Chapter 7, capturing the key RAG and Agentic RAG use cases across industries:

Table: RAG and Agentic RAG Use Cases by Industry

INDUSTRY	USE CASE	DESCRIPTION	RAG TYPE
HEALTHCARE	Clinical Decision Support	Retrieves up-to-date clinical guidelines and tailors them to patient records.	Agentic RAG
	Medical Research Assistant	Performs multi-hop search over PubMed and synthesizes summaries from multiple studies.	Agentic RAG
	Patient-Facing Health Chatbots	Provides personalized, HIPAA-compliant explanations of lab reports and care instructions.	RAG
	Drug Discovery and Trial Analysis	Extracts key insights from trial data and biomedical papers to assist in compound evaluation.	RAG
	Insurance Pre-Auth Assist	Retrieves payer-specific pre-authorization rules and assists providers in justifying medical necessity.	RAG
FINANCE	Agentic Risk Analysis	Iteratively pulls filings, trends, macro data, and historical events to assess exposure.	Agentic RAG
	Personalized Financial Advisory	Integrates user portfolios with real-time stock/ETF trends to offer tailored advice.	RAG
	Fraud Detection Reports	Flags anomalies by comparing transaction flows with compliance and KYC regulations.	RAG
	Regulatory Compliance Monitoring	Continuously scans new SEC/FINRA rules and highlights policy mismatches.	Agentic RAG
	Credit Underwriting Intelligence	Retrieves and contextualizes credit scores, spending behavior, and industry risk to support loan decisions.	RAG

RESEARCH / KNOWLEDGE WORK	Scientific Discovery	Performs multi-domain search and hypothesis generation across disparate research fields.	Agentic RAG
	Enterprise Knowledge Assistant	Retrieves answers across wikis, tickets, and internal documents.	RAG
	Patent and Legal Research	Tracks prior art and summarizes rulings or claim history.	RAG
	R&D Trend Forecasting	Combines academic literature with market and patent trends to highlight R&D gaps.	Agentic RAG
	Academic Paper Writing Assistant	Suggests citations, summarizes prior work, and auto-generates literature reviews.	RAG
E-COMMERCE	Hyper-Personalized Recommendations	Uses browsing history, product metadata, and reviews for tailored suggestions.	RAG
	Customer Support Chatbots	Answers product, warranty, return, and FAQ questions using policy documents and manuals.	RAG
	Dynamic Content Generation	Writes product descriptions and SEO content using inventory + trend data.	BART-RAG
	Voice/Visual Search Augmentation	Enhances product search with semantic image/voice retrieval.	Agentic RAG
	Post-Purchase Engagement	Provides order tracking, usage tips, and contextual upsells based on prior orders.	RAG
MEDIA & PUBLISHING	Fact-Checked Journalism	Verifies claims by retrieving evidence from reputable sources.	RAG
	Creative Writing Assistant	Aids journalists or authors in ideation and narrative generation.	BART-RAG
	Multi-Source News Summarization	Aggregates and distills articles from various sources into a coherent brief.	Agentic RAG
	Real-Time Event Tracking	Pulls updates from news feeds, social media, and press releases to monitor developing stories.	Agentic RAG

Chapter 8

A Glimpse into the Future: The Evolving Landscape of RAG Models

The field of Retrieval-Augmented Generation (RAG) is entering a transformative phase. While the foundational encoder–retriever–decoder framework remains powerful, the next generation of RAG models is poised to become autonomous, multimodal, and multilingual. These advancements will significantly broaden RAG's capabilities, making it a cornerstone of intelligent systems in 2025 and beyond.

8.1 Key Future Trends in RAG Models

1. Agentic RAG: Reasoning Meets Retrieval

The shift toward Agentic RAG represents a leap forward. Instead of a single retrieval step, Agentic RAG performs iterative reasoning and planning, acting like a self-directed research assistant.

What sets Agentic RAG apart:

- **Reason + Act Loops:** Inspired by frameworks like ReAct, Agentic RAG decides when to retrieve, when to reason, and when to finalize an answer.
- **Tool-Oriented Integration:** These systems can call APIs, run code, or access structured databases alongside unstructured document retrieval.
- **Complex Problem-Solving:** Capable of answering multi-step questions, performing analysis, and verifying results through multi-hop retrieval chains.

Example:
A corporate research assistant powered by Agentic RAG could analyze quarterly reports, cross-check stock market data, and draft strategic summaries in one continuous reasoning workflow.

2. Multilingual RAG: Breaking Language Barriers

Global enterprises and diverse user bases demand models that understand and generate multiple languages seamlessly.

- **Multilingual Retrieval:** RAG systems will fetch documents across different languages, translating and synthesizing content to provide a unified answer.

- **Use Case:** A multilingual RAG assistant could pull research from French, Japanese, and English medical journals to create a consolidated report in any target language.

3. Multimodal RAG: Beyond Text

The future of RAG will not be limited to text. **Multimodal RAG models will retrieve and generate insights from images, videos, audio, and structured data,** blending multiple content types.

- **Example:** A multimodal RAG assistant for product design could retrieve technical specifications (text), analyze diagrams (images), and summarize customer feedback (audio transcripts).

4. Continuous Learning and Real-Time Updates

- Future RAG models will integrate real-time data pipelines, ensuring outputs reflect the latest events or discoveries.
- **Lifelong Learning:** Systems will incrementally update their knowledge bases without full retraining, improving with every interaction.

5. Enhanced Explainability and Trust

As RAG models become more complex, explainable AI (XAI) features will be critical. Future RAG models will:

- Show which documents were retrieved and how they influenced the final output.
- Provide **confidence scores and evidence citations** for each generated answer.

8.2 The Rise of Agentic and Hybrid Workflows

Agentic RAG is expected to merge with other AI paradigms, such as:

- **Tool-Calling Agents:** RAG models enhanced with the ability to execute queries in SQL databases, spreadsheets, or APIs.
- **Hybrid RAG Systems:** Combining structured knowledge (graphs, tables) with unstructured retrieval, creating holistic answers.
- **Collaborative AI:** Systems where multiple specialized agents (researcher, summarizer, validator) work together to produce a single high-quality response.

8.3 Future Use Cases of RAG

- **Healthcare:** Autonomous RAG systems that plan clinical research reviews, combining diagnostic imaging, lab results, and latest studies.
- **Finance:** Real-time market intelligence platforms that monitor economic indicators, news feeds, and analyst reports simultaneously.
- **Education:** AI tutors that retrieve academic content, generate interactive lessons, and explain concepts in multiple modalities and languages.

8.4 Challenges Ahead

While the future of RAG is promising, several challenges must be addressed:

- **Latency & Cost:** Multi-hop and multimodal retrieval will increase computational demands.
- **Data Quality & Bias:** Ensuring retrieved content is accurate and unbiased remains a priority.
- **Evaluation Metrics:** Measuring the performance of reasoning-driven and multimodal systems requires new benchmarks.

Key Takeaways from Chapter 8

Agentic RAG will define the next wave of autonomous, reasoning-capable RAG systems.

Multilingual and multimodal RAG will expand applications across global and cross-media contexts.

The future of RAG is real-time, explainable, and deeply integrated with external tools and data sources.

Chapter 9

Open Collaboration: Exploring Community Contributions and Open-Source Innovations

The rapid growth of Retrieval-Augmented Generation (RAG) has been fueled not just by major research labs but also by open-source communities, startups, and collaborative ecosystems. As of 2025, open-source frameworks and tools have made it easier than ever to experiment, customize, and deploy RAG models at scale.

9.1 The Role of Open-Source in RAG Evolution

Open-source contributions have democratized RAG development by:

- Providing ready-to-use frameworks like LangChain, Haystack, and LlamaIndex that simplify pipeline building.
- Enabling plug-and-play retrievers and vector databases (e.g., FAISS, Milvus, Weaviate).
- Accelerating fine-tuning techniques, through shared datasets and pre-trained encoder/decoder models.

Example: LangChain's integration with vector stores and tool APIs allows developers to prototype RAG-powered agents in hours instead of weeks.

9.2 Key Open-Source Tools for RAG

1. Retrieval Frameworks

- LangChain: Provides modular building blocks for retrieval, reasoning, and agentic loops.
- Haystack: Focuses on enterprise-ready search and question answering.
- LlamaIndex: Optimized for ingesting and querying large document sets.

2. Vector Databases

- FAISS: Facebook AI Similarity Search, a highly efficient library for dense vector search.
- Pinecone & Milvus: Scalable, cloud-native solutions for real-time retrieval.

- **Qdrant & Weaviate:** Open-source vector databases with semantic search capabilities and hybrid filtering.

3. Open-Source Models

- **Hugging Face Hub:** Hosts community-trained RAG models, encoders (e.g., Sentence Transformers), and decoders (e.g., BART, T5).
- **LLaMA 2 and Mistral:** Open-weight LLMs that integrate seamlessly into RAG pipelines.
- **InstructorXL & E5 Models:** Pre-trained embedding models designed for high retrieval accuracy.

9.3 Community-Led Advancements

Open-source communities have contributed innovations such as:

- **Agentic RAG Templates:** Pre-built workflows that combine multi-hop retrieval with planning and tool use.
- **Benchmarking Suites:** Tools like RAGAS and BEIR datasets allow developers to evaluate retrieval quality and generation accuracy.
- **Shared Datasets:** Large corpora (e.g., PubMed abstracts, legal cases, financial filings) curated and released for public RAG experiments.

9.4 Collaboration with Industry and Research

- **Research Labs:** Academic groups are releasing state-of-the-art retrievers and hybrid pipelines under permissive licenses.
- **Industry Initiatives:** Companies like Cohere, Hugging Face, and OpenAI collaborate with the community to provide API-driven RAG solutions and fine-tuning tools.
- **Hackathons & Developer Communities:** Open hackathons (e.g., Hugging Face x LangChain) encourage rapid prototyping of Agentic RAG solutions, ranging from scientific literature summarizers to enterprise chat assistants.

9.5 The Rise of Open Agentic RAG

As Agentic RAG grows, open-source projects are focusing on:

- **Multi-Tool Integration:** Combining RAG with code execution, SQL querying, and API calls.
- **Transparent Reasoning:** Logging and displaying the agent's intermediate steps for explainability.
- **Agent-Oriented Frameworks:** Projects like LangGraph (LangChain's graph-based agent planner) are pioneering agentic RAG workflows.

9.6 Future Outlook for Open Collaboration

By 2025, open-source will continue to:

- Bridge the gap between cutting-edge research and real-world applications.
- Enable low-cost experimentation with RAG and agentic architectures for startups.
- Evolve toward community-driven hybrid RAG pipelines that are customizable, multimodal, and multilingual.

Key Takeaways from Chapter 9

Open-source tools like LangChain, Haystack, and LlamaIndex have made RAG experimentation accessible to all.

Community contributions (datasets, templates, benchmarks) accelerate innovation and adoption.

Agentic RAG is gaining momentum in open-source projects, offering autonomous reasoning and multi-hop retrieval out of the box.

Chapter 10

Empowering Performance: Leveraging Vector Databases in RAG Models

Retrieval is the heart of RAG models. No matter how powerful the language generator, the quality and speed of document retrieval directly influence accuracy, response time, and overall user experience. As of 2024–2025, vector databases (VDBs) have emerged as the backbone of scalable RAG pipelines, offering semantic search capabilities and support for hybrid retrieval strategies.

10.1 Why Vector Databases Matter

Traditional keyword-based search engines (like Elasticsearch) rely on exact term matches, which often fail to capture semantic meaning. In contrast, vector databases use dense embeddings (vector representations of text) to measure semantic similarity between queries and documents.

Benefits of Vector Databases for RAG:

- **Semantic Understanding:** Finds results based on meaning, not just keyword overlap.
- **Scalability:** Can store and search millions to billions of embeddings efficiently.
- **Real-Time Updates:** Support for incremental updates, enabling live knowledge bases.
- **Cross-Modal Retrieval:** Can store embeddings for text, images, and audio, enabling multimodal RAG.

10.2 Popular Vector Databases for RAG

1. **FAISS (Facebook AI Similarity Search):**
   - Open-source library optimized for large-scale dense vector search.
   - Offers GPU acceleration and fast k-NN (k-nearest neighbor) search.
2. **Milvus:**
   - Cloud-native and highly scalable, built for handling billions of vectors.
   - Ideal for enterprise deployments.

3. Pinecone:
    o Fully managed vector database with low-latency queries.
    o Popular for rapid prototyping and production deployments.
4. Weaviate & Qdrant:
    o Open-source VDBs supporting hybrid search (dense + keyword), filters, and semantic graph extensions.
    o Feature built-in APIs for RAG integration.

10.3 2024–2025 Trends in Vector Search

1. Hybrid Retrieval Systems

Modern RAG pipelines often combine dense embeddings (for semantic relevance) with sparse keyword search (for precision and keyword matching).

- **Example:** A hybrid retriever might first filter documents by keyword (using BM25), then rank them using vector similarity.

2. Multimodal Vector Storage

Emerging vector databases now handle **image embeddings (CLIP)**, **audio embeddings**, and structured data vectors.

- **Use Case:** A multimodal RAG assistant can retrieve a product image, its description, and user reviews simultaneously.

3. Vector Compression & Quantization

To handle billions of vectors efficiently, quantization techniques reduce memory footprint while preserving accuracy.

4. Native Integration with Agentic RAG

Agentic RAG systems perform iterative retrieval and require fast, low-latency queries. Vector databases now support **streaming retrieval** and **dynamic indexing** for agentic loops.

10.4 Designing a High-Performance Vector Search for RAG

Key Factors for Optimal Setup:

- **Embedding Model Quality:** Use domain-tuned encoders (e.g., biomedical embeddings for healthcare).
- **Chunking Strategy:** Split documents into semantic chunks to improve retrieval granularity.
- **Index Structures:** Use HNSW (Hierarchical Navigable Small World graphs) or IVF (Inverted File Index) for faster nearest-neighbor search.
- **Reranking:** Employ cross-encoders to rerank retrieved candidates for the most contextually accurate results.

10.5 Example: RAG + Vector Database Workflow

Scenario: A financial analyst asks, *"Summarize the impact of AI on global banking trends in 2024."*

1. **Query Encoding:** The question is embedded using a transformer (e.g., InstructorXL).
2. **Vector Search:** Pinecone retrieves top 10 semantically relevant documents (e.g., financial reports, AI trend papers).
3. **Reranking:** A cross-encoder filters results for relevance.
4. **Generation:** The decoder (e.g., BART or GPT) synthesizes a summary.

Key Takeaways from Chapter 10

Vector databases are central to the performance and accuracy of RAG models.

Hybrid retrieval (dense + sparse) is becoming standard for enterprise use cases.

The future of RAG involves multimodal, scalable, and agentic retrieval pipelines with vector databases at their core.

Chapter 11

Mastering Data Processing: Optimizing RAG Models Through Chunking

The quality of document retrieval in a RAG model is not just determined by the retriever or vector database it's heavily influenced by how information is chunked before indexing. Poorly designed chunks can lead to irrelevant or incomplete results, while smart chunking maximizes both precision and recall.

As of 2024–2025, chunking has evolved beyond fixed-length splits to semantic, context-aware, and adaptive strategies. These innovations ensure that retrieved segments preserve meaning and coherence, improving the accuracy of the generated responses.

11.1 Why Chunking Matters in RAG

- **Improved Retrieval Accuracy:** Smaller, well-structured chunks ensure that the retriever indexes meaningful units of text.
- **Reduced Context Loss:** Splitting documents into context-preserving chunks prevents the model from retrieving incomplete sentences or broken concepts.
- **Optimized Token Usage:** A good chunking strategy ensures maximum information density within the token limit of the language model.

11.2 Traditional vs. Advanced Chunking

Traditional approaches often split text into fixed token lengths (e.g., 512 tokens). While simple, this can break logical sentences or topics, leading to irrelevant retrieval results.

Advanced Chunking (2024–2025) introduces:

- **Semantic Chunking:** Uses AI to split text by meaning, not length.
- **Adaptive Windowing:** Dynamically adjusts chunk sizes based on document complexity and query context.
- **Vector Compression:** Reduces embedding redundancy to store more content without sacrificing retrieval quality.

11.3 Semantic Chunking

What It Is:
Semantic chunking divides documents into segments based on topic boundaries, headings, or meaning units rather than arbitrary length.

How It Works:

- Uses embedding-based similarity or NLP techniques to detect sentence-level coherence.
- Merges or splits content so that each chunk contains a complete thought or concept.

Example:
An academic paper might be split into "Abstract," "Methodology," "Results," and "Discussion" chunks, each embedding-rich and contextually complete.

Benefits:

- Reduces the risk of irrelevant retrieval.
- Improves answer grounding since the retrieved chunk directly addresses the query.

11.4 Adaptive Windowing

What It Is:
Instead of splitting content into fixed-length windows, adaptive windowing dynamically adjusts chunk size based on document complexity and query intent.

How It Works:

- If a query requires fine-grained details, the model uses smaller windows for precise retrieval.
- For broader context, larger chunks are indexed to capture holistic answers.

Use Case:
In customer support, adaptive windowing can generate short, direct troubleshooting snippets for FAQs while retrieving longer knowledge base entries for deep troubleshooting.

11.5 Vector Compression

Why It's Needed:
RAG models that deal with **millions of documents** face **storage and latency** challenges due to large embedding vectors.

Techniques:

- **Quantization:** Reducing vector precision (e.g., from 32-bit to 8-bit floats).
- **Dimensionality Reduction:** Using PCA or neural methods to compress embeddings while preserving semantic integrity.
- **Clustering & Deduplication:** Grouping similar vectors to avoid redundant storage.

2025 Trend:
Next-gen vector databases (e.g., Milvus 2.0, Pinecone Hybrid Index) natively integrate vector compression and semantic deduplication, enabling ultra-fast retrieval with lower costs.

11.6 Best Practices for Chunking in RAG

1. **Align Chunk Size with Model Context Window:**
   For GPT-4 or similar LLMs (8k–32k tokens), chunks of 200–400 tokens balance retrieval efficiency and relevance.
2. **Preserve Metadata:**
   Always store document metadata (e.g., titles, source URLs) along with embeddings for explainability and citations.
3. **Hybrid Indexing:**
   Use both semantic chunks and keyword indexes to ensure no critical keyword matches are missed.
4. **Iterative Testing:**
   Experiment with chunk sizes, overlap, and indexing strategies to optimize recall and precision metrics.

11.7 Real-World Example: Chunking for a Legal RAG Assistant

Scenario: A legal firm indexes 500k case files.

- **Step 1:** The system applies semantic chunking to separate case summaries, legal arguments, and judgments.
- **Step 2:** Adaptive windowing ensures longer judgments are split at logical breakpoints.

- Step 3: Vectors are compressed using quantization, reducing storage by 60% without losing search accuracy.
- Result: The assistant retrieves precise case snippets within milliseconds for complex queries like *"precedents in intellectual property disputes after 2022."*

11.8 Future of Chunking

- Automated Semantic Splitters: Tools powered by Agentic RAG will dynamically adjust chunking strategies during runtime based on query intent.
- Cross-Modal Chunking: Splitting image captions, audio transcripts, and videos into retrievable segments for multimodal RAG.
- Self-Optimizing Pipelines: Retrieval systems will relearn optimal chunk sizes by analyzing query-response performance over time.

Key Takeaways from Chapter 11

Semantic chunking ensures retrieval is meaning-driven rather than token-driven.

Adaptive windowing dynamically optimizes retrieval for different use cases.

Vector compression and hybrid strategies will define 2024–2025 RAG scalability.

Chapter 12

Fine-Tuning Techniques: Unlocking the Full Potential of RAG Models

While retrieval plays a critical role in RAG pipelines, the generation quality depends on how well the underlying language model is aligned with the task, domain, and tone. Fine-tuning ensures that RAG models are not just accurate but also adapted to specific industries or workflows.

In 2025, the most impactful fine-tuning approaches for RAG include RAFT fine-tuning, low-rank adaptation (LoRA), and instruction tuning. These techniques are efficient, cost-effective, and optimized for large-scale RAG deployments.

12.1 Why Fine-Tuning Matters in RAG

- **Domain Adaptation:** Out-of-the-box models lack the specialized knowledge required for domains like healthcare, finance, or legal research. Fine-tuning bridges this gap.
- **Improved Answer Relevance:** By aligning generation with retrieval style and domain language, responses become more precise and professional.
- **Consistency:** Fine-tuned models maintain coherent tone and terminology across tasks.

12.2 RAFT Fine-Tuning: Retrieval-Aware Fine-Tuning

What It Is:
RAFT (Retrieval-Augmented Fine-Tuning) optimizes both the retriever and the generator jointly, improving how the model integrates retrieved content into responses.

How It Works:

1. **Retriever Tuning:** Embedding models are fine-tuned on domain-specific query-document pairs.
2. **Generation Tuning:** The generator learns to produce context-aware, retrieval-grounded outputs based on retrieved chunks.
3. **Alignment:** RAFT ensures retrieved content and generated answers complement each other rather than being disjointed.

Use Case Example:

- In healthcare RAG, RAFT fine-tuning ensures the model prioritizes recent clinical guidelines and accurately integrates them into patient care summaries.

Benefits:

- Boosted precision and recall.
- Reduced hallucinations as the model learns to rely on retrieved facts.
- Seamless retriever-generator alignment.

12.3 Low-Rank Adaptation (LoRA): Efficient Fine-Tuning

What It Is:
LoRA is a parameter-efficient fine-tuning technique that adapts large models by updating only a small set of low-rank matrices while keeping the majority of parameters frozen.

Why It's Perfect for RAG:

- Large language models used in RAG (like GPT or BART) are expensive to retrain.
- LoRA allows fine-tuning on smaller datasets with significant cost savings.

Example:

- A financial RAG assistant can be fine-tuned with LoRA to use industry jargon (e.g., "yield curve inversion") without retraining the entire model.

Benefits:

- Up to 10x faster fine-tuning compared to full model training.
- Allows for multiple domain-specific adapters (e.g., healthcare vs. legal) on the same base model.

12.4 Instruction Tuning for RAG

What It Is:
Instruction tuning teaches the model to follow specific instructions or task formats, making responses more aligned with user intent.

How It Works:

- Uses instruction-response pairs (e.g., "Summarize this document with 3 key points" → response).
- Fine-tunes the model to respond to task-specific prompts consistently.

RAG-Specific Enhancement:

- Instruction tuning ensures the generator utilizes retrieved content correctly and answers in the style required (e.g., concise executive summaries vs. detailed technical explanations).

Example:

- A research RAG system might be instruction-tuned to always cite sources retrieved during generation, increasing trust and explainability.

12.5 Combining RAFT, LoRA, and Instruction Tuning

Modern RAG solutions often use a hybrid fine-tuning strategy:

1. RAFT aligns retrieval with generation.
2. LoRA provides cost-efficient domain adaptation.
3. Instruction tuning ensures task-specific and user-friendly outputs.

Use Case:
A legal RAG assistant might use RAFT to retrieve precedents, LoRA to understand legal terminology, and instruction tuning to summarize judgments in lawyer-friendly language.

12.6 2024–2025 Fine-Tuning Trends

- **Domain-Specific Mini-RAG Models:** Smaller, LoRA-fine-tuned RAG models focused on niche verticals (e.g., radiology, tax law).
- **Agentic Fine-Tuning:** Training models to better plan multi-step retrieval loops (critical for Agentic RAG).
- **Continual Fine-Tuning:** Updating models incrementally with real-time datasets while avoiding catastrophic forgetting.

12.7 Best Practices for Fine-Tuning RAG Models

- **Use High-Quality Domain Data:** Fine-tuning on noisy or irrelevant datasets harms retrieval-grounded responses.
- **Start Small with LoRA:** Avoid full model training unless absolutely necessary.
- **Validate Outputs:** Use human-in-the-loop evaluations to ensure domain accuracy.
- **Leverage Community Datasets:** Open-source instruction-tuning datasets (e.g., Dolly, Alpaca) can be adapted for RAG.

Key Takeaways from Chapter 12

RAFT improves retrieval-generation synergy.

LoRA delivers efficient, low-cost fine-tuning for large RAG models.

Instruction tuning ensures outputs align with user needs and domain style.

The future of fine-tuning will combine parameter-efficient methods with agentic reasoning loops for next-gen RAG systems.

Appendix

This appendix section enriches the main content, offering deeper insights into RAG models, their architecture, applications, and resources for further exploration.

Foundational Concepts and Comparisons

- **IR vs RAG:** Delve into the evolution from traditional Information Retrieval (IR) to advanced RAG models, highlighting the integration of retrieval with generative models for enhanced performance.
- **RAG Architecture Components:** Explore the components that constitute RAG models, understanding their construction and functionality.
- **Choosing the Right Platform and Tools for Your Project:** choosing among cloud providers like AWS, GCP, Azure, open-source solutions, and specialized tools, aligning these choices with the project's unique demands and aspirations
- **Technology Stack for RAG Architecture:** detailed guide for selecting the right tools and features, tailored to the specific needs and complexity of your project

Comparative Analyses and Use Cases

- **RAG Model Variants:** A comparative analysis of RAG model variants, focusing on their strengths and optimal use cases.
- **Applications Across Industries:** Discover how RAG models are applied in various industries, showcasing their versatility and impact.

Technical Resources and Code

- Code Snippets and Resource Links: Access a curated collection of code examples, tutorials, and resources for practical engagement with RAG models.

Information Retrieval (IR) vs. Retrieval-Augmented Generation (RAG): A Clear Distinction

While **Information Retrieval (IR)** and **Retrieval-Augmented Generation (RAG)** share the common goal of finding relevant information, they operate at fundamentally different levels of intelligence and user experience. This section clarifies how RAG builds upon and extends the capabilities of traditional IR systems.

A.1 What Is Information Retrieval (IR)?

Definition:
Information Retrieval refers to the process of searching and retrieving documents or data from a collection, based on a user query. Traditional IR systems do not generate new content; they return ranked lists of documents or passages for the user to interpret.

Examples of IR Systems:

- Search engines (Google, Bing).
- Document search tools (ElasticSearch, BM25-based enterprise search).
- Library catalog search.

Key Characteristics of IR:

- **Keyword Matching:** IR systems rely heavily on exact word matches, often missing semantic relevance.
- **No Synthesis:** The user must read retrieved documents to form their own answers.
- **Limited Context Awareness:** IR systems treat queries as standalone strings, lacking deep contextual understanding.

A.2 What Is RAG?

Definition:
Retrieval-Augmented Generation (RAG) integrates IR-like retrieval with natural language generation (NLG). Instead of simply returning documents, RAG models:

1. Retrieve relevant content from a knowledge base.

2. Synthesize a natural language answer by merging the retrieved data with the user's query.

Examples of RAG Systems:

- AI assistants that provide factually grounded answers (e.g., ChatGPT + retrieval plug-ins).
- Domain-specific bots that reference company wikis or research papers.
- Agentic RAG systems that iteratively plan, retrieve, and generate answers.

A.3 Core Differences: IR vs. RAG

ASPECT	INFORMATION RETRIEVAL (IR)	RETRIEVAL-AUGMENTED GENERATION (RAG)
OUTPUT	Ranked documents or excerpts	Fluent, synthesized answers
CONTEXT AWARENESS	Limited – query treated as keywords	High – combines user query with retrieved context
CONTENT GENERATION	None – user interprets results	Generates natural language responses
SEMANTIC UNDERSTANDING	Often keyword-based	Embedding-based semantic retrieval + reasoning
USER EFFORT	High – user must parse multiple sources	Low – RAG summarizes and contextualizes results
APPLICATIONS	Search engines, document retrieval	Q&A bots, enterprise assistants, research agents

A.4 Why RAG Is the Next Step Beyond IR

- **Combines Search and Synthesis:** RAG performs both retrieval (like IR) and generation (like LLMs), creating ready-to-use insights.
- **Factuality and Freshness:** By pulling real-time data, RAG models reduce hallucinations compared to standalone language models.
- **Versatility:** RAG can handle both structured (SQL, APIs) and unstructured content (documents, PDFs), whereas IR is mostly text-based.

A.5 IR + RAG: A Hybrid Future

In 2025 and beyond, IR and RAG are becoming complementary rather than competitive:

- **IR Powers RAG:** Vector databases and ranking algorithms from IR form the retrieval layer for RAG systems.
- **Hybrid Search Pipelines:** Enterprises combine keyword-based filtering with semantic RAG retrieval for optimal performance.
- **Agentic RAG:** Next-gen assistants use IR components as tools for multi-hop retrieval in reasoning loops.

Key Takeaway

While IR retrieves information for the user, RAG retrieves and interprets information with the user, bridging the gap between search and intelligent content creation.

RAG Architecture components

Dissecting the RAG Architecture: Key Components Explained

A Retrieval-Augmented Generation (RAG) system is composed of three interconnected modules the Encoder, Retriever, and Decoder orchestrated in a pipeline that transforms a user's query into a factually grounded, natural language answer. This section provides a deep dive into each component and the workflow, including variations in modern (2024–2025) RAG architectures.

B.1 The RAG Workflow Overview

At a high level, RAG follows these stages:

1. **Query Encoding** – The user's question is transformed into a semantic vector.
2. **Document Retrieval** – Relevant chunks are fetched from a vector database or hybrid index.
3. **Context Integration** – Retrieved documents are packaged with the original query.
4. **Answer Generation** – The decoder generates a response that merges retrieved facts with natural language fluency.

B.2 Key Components of RAG

1. Encoder – The Interpreter

- **Purpose:** Converts text (queries, documents) into dense vector embeddings that represent semantic meaning.
- **Popular Models:** BERT, Sentence Transformers, or domain-tuned encoders (e.g., **BioBERT** for medical text).
- **Advancements (2025):**
    - Encoders optimized for multi-modal retrieval (text + images).
    - Instruction-aware encoders that consider the *task context* for improved retrieval precision.

---

2. Retriever – The Knowledge Seeker

- **Purpose:** Finds the most semantically relevant chunks from the knowledge base.

- Types of Retrieval:
  - Sparse Retrieval: BM25 or keyword-based filters.
  - Dense Retrieval: Vector similarity search using FAISS, Pinecone, Milvus, or Qdrant.
  - Hybrid Retrieval: A combination of both, often used in enterprise RAG.
- Modern Enhancements:
  - Contextual Reranking: Cross-encoders refine the ranking of retrieved documents.
  - Multi-hop Retrieval: Iterative search steps for complex queries (e.g., Agentic RAG loops).

---

3. Decoder – The Storyteller

- Purpose: Synthesizes information from both the user query and retrieved documents to generate a fluent, accurate answer.
- Common Models: BART, T5, GPT-based models, or open-weight models like LLaMA 2.
- Advanced Features (2025):
  - Fact Attribution: The decoder can highlight which document supports each answer segment.
  - Instruction-tuned decoders for domain-specific tone and structured outputs.

B.3 Agentic Extensions to RAG

With Agentic RAG, this pipeline becomes dynamic:

- The retriever is called iteratively as the agent refines its understanding.
- Tools like LangChain Agents or LangGraph add planning and reasoning steps, making retrieval goal-oriented rather than a single static pass.

B.4 RAG Pipeline Diagram

Below is a conceptual diagram illustrating a modern RAG workflow:

User Query → [Encoder] → [Retriever] ↔ [Vector Database] → [Context Packager] → [Decoder] → Answer Generation

For **Agentic RAG**, an additional **Reasoning Loop** (Plan → Retrieve → Evaluate → Refine) wraps around the retriever and decoder.

B.5 Agentic RAG Within the Pipeline

With Agentic RAG, the pipeline becomes iterative rather than linear:

- After the first generation, the **agentic loop** decides whether additional retrieval is needed (e.g., to fill missing details).
- **Planning modules** (such as reasoning frameworks like ReAct or LangChain agents) can dynamically query multiple data sources, improving accuracy for complex tasks.

B.6 Orchestrating the Knowledge Flow

A robust RAG system requires:

- **Preprocessing Pipelines:** Document cleaning, tokenization, and chunking for retrieval indexing.
- **Embedding Store Management:** Efficient indexing of documents and periodic updates to keep knowledge fresh.
- **Ranking Algorithms:** Post-retrieval ranking (e.g., via cross-encoders) to filter out low-quality results.
- **Caching:** Frequently accessed queries can be cached for speed, reducing retrieval costs.

B.7 Real-World Example: RAG in Legal Tech

Consider a legal assistant powered by RAG:

1. **Query:** "Summarize the latest precedent on intellectual property disputes."
2. **Encoding:** Query is embedded and sent to a legal document index.
3. **Retrieval:** The system fetches relevant case law and recent judgments.
4. **Generation:** The decoder merges retrieved content and produces a legally accurate, citation-backed summary.

B.8 Challenges in RAG Pipelines

- **Context Window Limits:** Large documents must be chunked into smaller sections, risking the loss of key context.
- **Latency:** Multi-step retrieval can slow down response time.
- **Evaluation:** Balancing retrieval quality and generation fluency requires new metrics like **RAGAS** (RAG Assessment Scores).

Choosing the Right Platform and Tools for Your Project

Building a robust RAG (Retrieval-Augmented Generation) solution involves selecting the right combination of platforms, frameworks, and databases that align with your business goals, data requirements, and scalability needs. With the 2024–2025 advancements in AI infrastructure, developers have a rich ecosystem of tools for retrieval, orchestration, and generation.

C.1 Key Considerations When Selecting Tools

1. **Data Scale and Complexity**
   - Small to Medium Projects: A lightweight vector database like Qdrant or Weaviate combined with open-source models can suffice.
   - Enterprise-Grade Solutions: Managed services like Pinecone, Milvus Cloud, or ElasticSearch + Dense Vectors provide higher scalability and uptime guarantees.
2. **Domain Requirements**
   - For healthcare or finance, choose platforms supporting compliance and data privacy (e.g., HIPAA/GDPR-ready).
   - Use domain-tuned encoders (e.g., BioBERT for medical, LegalBERT for legal tasks).
3. **Cost and Efficiency**
   - Parameter-efficient methods like LoRA fine-tuning reduce infrastructure costs.
   - Choose platforms with pay-as-you-go pricing (e.g., managed vector databases).
4. **Integration Flexibility**
   - Frameworks like LangChain and LlamaIndex integrate easily with LLMs, vector stores, and APIs.
   - Agentic RAG projects benefit from LangGraph or orchestration layers that handle multi-step reasoning loops.

C.2 Recommended Platforms for RAG Projects (2024–2025)

COMPONENT	RECOMMENDED TOOLS	WHY USE IT?
RETRIEVAL FRAMEWORKS	LangChain, Haystack, LlamaIndex	Modular pipelines, agentic workflows, multi-hop search
VECTOR DATABASES	FAISS, Milvus, Pinecone, Qdrant, Weaviate	Fast, scalable semantic search with hybrid support
LLM DECODERS	OpenAI GPT-4/4o, Anthropic Claude 3, LLaMA 2, Mistral	High-quality natural language generation
ORCHESTRATION	LangChain Agents, LangGraph, OpenAI Function Calling	Tool use and reasoning automation
EMBEDDING MODELS	OpenAI text-embedding-3, InstructorXL, E5, Cohere Embed	State-of-the-art vector embeddings
EVALUATION	RAGAS, BEIR, LangChain Evaluation Suite	Retrieval and generation performance benchmarking

C.3 Tool Stacks for Different Project Sizes

1. Prototype / MVP:

- Framework: LangChain or LlamaIndex.
- Database: Qdrant or Weaviate (local setup).
- LLM: OpenAI GPT-4o (API-based) or Hugging Face open models.
- Focus: Fast iteration and proof-of-concept.

2. Mid-Scale Product:

- Framework: Haystack or LangChain.
- Database: Pinecone or Milvus Cloud for larger datasets.
- LLM: Fine-tuned BART or LLaMA 2 with LoRA.
- Focus: Performance, domain adaptation, and cost optimization.

3. Enterprise Deployment:

- Framework: LangChain Agents + LangGraph for agentic workflows.
- Database: Pinecone Enterprise or hybrid search (ElasticSearch + FAISS).

- **LLM:** Combination of OpenAI GPT + on-prem models for sensitive data.
- **Focus:** Scalability, security, compliance.

C.4 Trends for 2025

- **Agentic RAG-Oriented Stacks:** Frameworks now natively support multi-hop retrieval, tool calls, and planning (e.g., LangChain + LangGraph).
- **Multimodal Support:** Weaviate and Milvus offer native storage of text, image, and audio embeddings for multimodal RAG.
- **Serverless RAG Services:** Managed services like Pinecone Serverless reduce infrastructure complexity.

Key Takeaways

Choose tools based on project size, data sensitivity, and scalability needs.

For Agentic RAG, prioritize frameworks that support planning, reasoning, and tool integration.

Future RAG pipelines will be multimodal, cloud-native, and powered by open-source + enterprise hybrid stacks.

Technology Stack for RAG Architecture

Building Your RAG Project: Essential Technology Stack

A successful RAG implementation is built on a carefully chosen technology stack that balances retrieval accuracy, generation quality, and scalability. In this section, we outline end-to-end architecture templates for small-scale prototypes, mid-level products, and enterprise deployments (2025).

D.1 Core Components of a RAG Stack

A typical RAG technology stack includes:

- **Frontend Layer:** Chat interface, API endpoints, or web application.
- **Retrieval Layer:** Vector databases or hybrid search engines for document retrieval.
- **Embedding Models:** Transformer-based models for encoding queries and documents.
- **Language Model (Decoder):** A generative LLM (e.g., GPT, LLaMA, or BART).
- **Orchestration Framework:** Handles query processing, retrieval coordination, and agentic workflows (e.g., LangChain, LangGraph).
- **Evaluation & Monitoring Tools:** Metrics tracking, output validation, and logging.
- **Security & Compliance Layers:** Authentication, data encryption, and privacy controls.

D.2 Architecture Template for Small-Scale / Prototype RAG

Use Case: Proof-of-concept, startup MVPs, or academic projects.
Focus: Low-cost, quick deployment with minimal infrastructure.

Technology Stack:

- **Frontend:** Streamlit or Gradio-based UI.
- **Retrieval:** Local FAISS or Qdrant (lightweight, easy setup).
- **Embedding Model:** OpenAI text-embedding-3-small or Sentence Transformers.
- **LLM Decoder:** OpenAI GPT-4o or Hugging Face BART.
- **Framework:** LlamaIndex or LangChain for pipeline orchestration.
- **Hosting:** Single server or cloud VM (AWS EC2, Azure VM).

- **Evaluation:** Simple BLEU/ROUGE metrics or RAGAS for retrieval quality.

Flow:

1. Query → Encoder (Embedding).
2. FAISS/Qdrant retrieves top-k documents.
3. Decoder generates a response with retrieved context.
4. Results displayed via a simple web app.

D.3 Architecture Template for Mid-Level Product

Use Case: SaaS applications, domain-specific assistants, or medium-scale chatbots.
Focus: Higher performance, improved domain adaptation, and moderate scaling.

Technology Stack:

- **Frontend:** React/Next.js-based application.
- **Retrieval:** Milvus or Pinecone Serverless (handles millions of vectors).
- **Embedding Model:** Instructor XL or Cohere Embed (domain-tuned).
- **LLM Decoder:** Fine-tuned BART or LLaMA 2 13B with LoRA for cost efficiency.
- **Framework:** LangChain or Haystack for agentic retrieval loops.
- **Monitoring:** OpenTelemetry + LangSmith evaluation for chain performance.
- **Infrastructure:** Containerized deployment (Docker + Kubernetes).
- **Security:** Basic role-based access control, encrypted storage.

Flow:

1. Query processing and semantic embedding generation.
2. Vector retrieval using Milvus/Pinecone.
3. Context reranking with cross-encoder for precision.
4. Decoder (fine-tuned LLaMA/BART) generates a domain-optimized answer.
5. Logs and metrics fed into monitoring dashboards.

D.4 Architecture Template for Enterprise-Grade Deployment

Use Case: Fortune 500 organizations, regulated industries (healthcare, finance, legal).
Focus: Scalability, compliance, multi-modal retrieval, and agentic reasoning.

Technology Stack:

- Frontend: Custom enterprise portals or Teams/Slack bot integrations.
- Retrieval: Hybrid ElasticSearch + Pinecone/Milvus Enterprise, with multi-modal vector indexing (text, images, tables).
- Embedding Model: Domain-specific encoders (e.g., BioBERT, LegalBERT) + OpenAI text-embedding-3-large.
- LLM Decoder: GPT-4 Enterprise, Claude 3, or on-prem Mistral 8x7B clusters.
- Framework: LangChain Agents + LangGraph for multi-hop reasoning and tool use.
- Tool Integration: SQL databases, CRM/ERP connectors, API calling.
- Monitoring & Governance:
  - RAGAS + custom dashboards for output quality.
  - Human-in-the-loop verification for high-stakes tasks.
  - Compliance logging for HIPAA, SOC 2, or GDPR.
- Infrastructure: Kubernetes + Istio service mesh, private VPC (AWS, Azure, GCP), and vector compression for cost control.

Flow:

1. Agentic planner decomposes query into sub-tasks.
2. Hybrid retrievers (dense + keyword filters) fetch multimodal data.
3. Context merging + cross-checking for accuracy and citation.
4. LLM decoder outputs fact-grounded responses with evidence links.
5. Feedback loop for continual improvement (fine-tuning and retraining pipelines).

D.5 Trends in RAG Stacks for 2025

- Agentic Pipelines: Native support for multi-hop planning and tool orchestration.
- Multimodal Retrieval: Integrated handling of text, images, and structured data.
- Serverless RAG APIs: Pay-per-query solutions reducing DevOps overhead.
- Federated Knowledge Retrieval: Secure cross-database querying across private and public datasets.

Key Takeaways

Prototype stacks prioritize simplicity, while enterprise stacks emphasize compliance, scalability, and hybrid search.

Modern RAG platforms combine vector databases, agentic frameworks, and fine-tuned LLMs for high performance.

2025 RAG solutions lean heavily on orchestration frameworks (LangChain/LangGraph) for Agentic RAG workflows.

RAG Model Variants: A Comparative Overview of Strengths and Applications

Retrieval-Augmented Generation (RAG) has evolved from its baseline architecture (Naive RAG) to advanced, context-aware, and reasoning-driven models like Agentic RAG. Each variant is designed to meet specific requirements, ranging from simple Q&A to complex multi-step reasoning.

This section provides a side-by-side comparison of the major RAG variants: Naive RAG, Conditional RAG (C-RAG), Self-RAG, Dense RAG, BART-RAG, and Agentic RAG.

E.1 Overview of RAG Variants

1. Naive RAG

- **Definition:** The simplest RAG setup – retrieves documents based on the query and generates a response without contextual conditioning or reasoning.
- **Use Case:** General-purpose Q&A, document summarization.
- **Limitations:** Limited personalization or advanced reasoning.

2. Conditional RAG (C-RAG)

- **Definition:** Enhances retrieval by conditioning it on contextual cues (e.g., user preferences, task intent).
- **Use Case:** Personalized chatbots, context-aware assistants.
- **Strength:** Tailors retrieval to the specific context.

3. Self-RAG

- **Definition:** Uses its own previously generated outputs as an internal knowledge base for long-term memory and consistency.
- **Use Case:** Research assistants, conversational memory in chatbots.
- **Strength:** Builds incremental knowledge over time.

4. Dense RAG

- **Definition:** Focuses on semantic retrieval using dense embeddings (e.g., FAISS, Milvus).
- **Use Case:** Legal, biomedical, and scientific search where keyword matching fails.

- **Strength:** High retrieval precision due to semantic similarity search.

5. BART-RAG

- **Definition:** Uses BART as the decoder, resulting in more coherent, fluent, and structured responses.
- **Use Case:** Report writing, creative content, and structured summarization.
- **Strength:** Superior language fluency and narrative style.

6. Agentic RAG

- **Definition:** Integrates reasoning loops, planning, and multi-step retrieval with tool calling and advanced orchestration.
- **Use Case:** Research agents, autonomous data analysis, multi-hop question answering.
- **Strength:** Handles complex tasks requiring reasoning and multiple retrieval steps.

E.2 Comparative Table of RAG Variants

VARIANT	FOCUS AREA	STRENGTHS	LIMITATIONS	BEST APPLICATIONS
NAIVE RAG	Basic retrieval + generation	Simple to set up, fast results	Limited context and reasoning	FAQ bots, simple Q&A, basic summarization
C-RAG	Context-aware retrieval	Personalization, domain adaptation	Needs well-defined context inputs	Chatbots, e-commerce assistants
SELF-RAG	Long-term memory	Builds consistency over time	Risk of self-propagating errors	Conversational agents, research tools
DENSE RAG	Semantic precision	High-quality retrieval, domain-focused	Higher compute/storage needs	Legal, biomedical, financial research
BART-RAG	Language fluency	More natural, creative responses	May over-emphasize style over fact	Reports, articles, narrative-based tasks
AGENTIC RAG	Multi-step reasoning	Iterative retrieval, tool integration	Latency & cost due to complexity	Research assistants, multi-hop reasoning tasks

E.3 Key Insights

- Naive RAG is ideal for quick deployments but lacks advanced contextual intelligence.
- C-RAG and Self-RAG shine when personalization or continuity is required.
- Dense RAG is preferred for high-stakes, domain-heavy search tasks (e.g., legal research).
- BART-RAG improves generation quality, making it suitable for human-readable summaries and reports.
- Agentic RAG is the future of RAG capable of reasoning, planning, and autonomous tool use.

Code Snippets and Resource Links: A Practical Guide

This section provides ready-to-use code snippets and essential resources to help you implement and experiment with RAG models quickly. The snippets cover key tasks such as document embedding, retrieval, and RAG pipeline orchestration using popular frameworks (LangChain, Hugging Face, and FAISS).

F.1 Basic RAG Pipeline with LangChain

```
# Install required libraries
!pip install langchain openai faiss-cpu tiktoken

from langchain.embeddings.openai import OpenAIEmbeddings
from langchain.vectorstores import FAISS
from langchain.chains import RetrievalQA
from langchain.chat_models import ChatOpenAI
from langchain.text_splitter import RecursiveCharacterTextSplitter

# Step 1: Load and split documents
text_splitter = RecursiveCharacterTextSplitter(chunk_size=500,
chunk_overlap=50)
texts = text_splitter.split_text("Your raw document content goes here...")

# Step 2: Create embeddings and store them in FAISS
embeddings = OpenAIEmbeddings(model="text-embedding-3-small")
vectorstore = FAISS.from_texts(texts, embeddings)

# Step 3: Initialize the RAG pipeline
qa_chain = RetrievalQA.from_chain_type(
    llm=ChatOpenAI(model_name="gpt-4", temperature=0),
    retriever=vectorstore.as_retriever()
)

# Step 4: Ask a question
query = "What are the key points from the document?"
response = qa_chain.run(query)
print(response)
```

F.2 Dense Retrieval with Sentence Transformers + FAISS

```
!pip install sentence-transformers faiss-cpu

from sentence_transformers import SentenceTransformer
```

```python
import faiss
import numpy as np

# Step 1: Load an embedding model
model = SentenceTransformer('all-MiniLM-L6-v2')

# Step 2: Create embeddings for documents
documents = ["Doc 1 text...", "Doc 2 text...", "Doc 3 text..."]
doc_embeddings = model.encode(documents)

# Step 3: Build FAISS index
dimension = doc_embeddings.shape[1]
index = faiss.IndexFlatL2(dimension)
index.add(np.array(doc_embeddings))

# Step 4: Perform retrieval
query = "Key insights from Doc 2?"
query_embedding = model.encode([query])
distances, indices = index.search(np.array(query_embedding), k=2)

# Display results
for idx in indices[0]:
    print(f"Retrieved: {documents[idx]}")
```

F.3 Hugging Face Transformers RAG Implementation

```python
!pip install transformers datasets

from transformers import RagTokenizer, RagRetriever, RagTokenForGeneration

# Initialize RAG components
tokenizer = RagTokenizer.from_pretrained("facebook/rag-token-nq")
retriever = RagRetriever.from_pretrained("facebook/rag-token-nq",
index_name="exact")
model = RagTokenForGeneration.from_pretrained("facebook/rag-token-nq")

# Query
query = "What is quantum computing?"
input_ids = tokenizer(query, return_tensors="pt").input_ids

# Generate answer
output = model.generate(input_ids)
print(tokenizer.batch_decode(output, skip_special_tokens=True))
```

F.4 Agentic RAG Example (LangChain Agents)

```python
from langchain.agents import initialize_agent, Tool
from langchain.chat_models import ChatOpenAI
```

```
from langchain.tools import WikipediaQueryRun
from langchain.utilities import WikipediaAPIWrapper

# LLM
llm = ChatOpenAI(temperature=0, model="gpt-4")

# Tool for retrieval
wiki = WikipediaQueryRun(api_wrapper=WikipediaAPIWrapper())

# Initialize Agentic RAG
agent = initialize_agent(
    tools=[Tool(name="Wikipedia", func=wiki.run, description="Useful for
looking up facts")],
    llm=llm,
    agent="zero-shot-react-description",
    verbose=True
)

response = agent.run("Find the history of quantum computing and summarize it in
3 bullet points.")
print(response)
```

F.5 Recommended Resource Links

Official Documentation & Frameworks

- LangChain Documentation
- Haystack by deepset
- LlamaIndex (formerly GPT Index)
- Hugging Face RAG Models

Vector Database Platforms

- FAISS (Facebook AI Similarity Search)
- Pinecone
- Weaviate
- Qdrant
- Milvus

Evaluation & Benchmarks

- RAGAS (RAG Assessment Suite)
- BEIR Benchmark

Key Takeaways

- Start with **LangChain or Hugging Face** for quick RAG prototyping.
- Use **FAISS or Pinecone** for scalable vector search.
- Explore **Agentic RAG frameworks** (LangChain Agents, LangGraph) for multi-step reasoning.
- Leverage open-source tools and datasets for fine-tuning and benchmarking.

Here's a **Starter RAG Project Template** – a single Python script that demonstrates how to:

- Load and chunk documents
- Create embeddings
- Store them in a vector database (FAISS)
- Run a simple Retrieval-Augmented Generation query using OpenAI GPT

Starter RAG Project Template (Python)

```python
# ============================================
# Starter RAG Project Template
# ============================================

# ---- Step 0: Install Required Packages ----
# !pip install openai langchain faiss-cpu tiktoken

import os
from langchain.embeddings.openai import OpenAIEmbeddings
from langchain.text_splitter import RecursiveCharacterTextSplitter
from langchain.vectorstores import FAISS
from langchain.chat_models import ChatOpenAI
from langchain.chains import RetrievalQA

# ============================================
# Step 1: Set Your API Key
# ============================================
# Replace with your OpenAI API key or set it as an environment variable
os.environ["OPENAI_API_KEY"] = "your-openai-api-key"

# ============================================
# Step 2: Load Your Documents
# ============================================
```

```python
# For demo purposes, we'll use a string. Replace this with file/document ingestion.
raw_text = """
Quantum computing leverages quantum bits (qubits) that can exist in multiple
states simultaneously,
offering exponential speedups for certain types of computations compared to
classical computers.
Post-quantum cryptography is an area of research developing encryption methods
resistant to quantum attacks.
"""


# ===================================================
# Step 3: Chunk Documents
# ===================================================
text_splitter = RecursiveCharacterTextSplitter(chunk_size=300,
chunk_overlap=50)
docs = text_splitter.split_text(raw_text)


# ===================================================
# Step 4: Create Embeddings and Vector Store
# ===================================================
embeddings = OpenAIEmbeddings(model="text-embedding-3-small")
vectorstore = FAISS.from_texts(docs, embeddings)


# ===================================================
# Step 5: Create RAG Pipeline (Retriever + Generator)
# ===================================================
qa_chain = RetrievalQA.from_chain_type(
    llm=ChatOpenAI(model_name="gpt-4", temperature=0),
    retriever=vectorstore.as_retriever(),
    return_source_documents=True
)


# ===================================================
# Step 6: Ask Questions
# ===================================================
query = "What is quantum computing and how does it impact cryptography?"
result = qa_chain({"query": query})


# ===================================================
# Step 7: Display Results
# ===================================================
print("\nQuestion:", query)
print("Answer:", result["result"])
print("\nSource Documents:")
for doc in result["source_documents"]:
    print("-", doc.page_content)
```

How This Script Works

1. Text Chunking: Splits large documents into smaller, context-preserving chunks (300 characters each).
2. Embeddings: Uses OpenAI's embedding model (text-embedding-3-small) to convert chunks into vector representations.
3. Vector Store: Stores embeddings in FAISS for fast similarity search.
4. Retrieval + Generation: Fetches the top-k relevant chunks and passes them to GPT-4 for a fact-grounded answer.
5. Result Display: Shows both the answer and the retrieved source documents.

Next Steps to Expand This Template

- Replace raw_text with PDF ingestion using langchain.document_loaders.PyPDFLoader.
- Add semantic chunking (Chapter 11 techniques).
- Integrate a vector database like Pinecone or Milvus for larger datasets.
- Include Agentic RAG loops with LangChain Agents for multi-step reasoning.

Here's an Advanced Agentic RAG Project Template, which adds multi-hop retrieval, tool integration, and step-by-step reasoning using LangChain Agents:

Advanced Agentic RAG Project Template (Python)

```python
# ===== ==== ==== ==== ==== ==== ==== ==== ==== =
# Advanced Agentic RAG Project Template
# ===== ==== ==== ==== ==== ==== ==== ==== ==== =


# ---- Step 0: Install Required Packages ----
# !pip install openai langchain faiss-cpu wikipedia tiktoken

import os
from langchain.chat_models import ChatOpenAI
from langchain.agents import initialize_agent, Tool
from langchain.chains import RetrievalQA
from langchain.embeddings.openai import OpenAIEmbeddings
from langchain.vectorstores import FAISS
from langchain.text_splitter import RecursiveCharacterTextSplitter
from langchain.utilities import WikipediaAPIWrapper


# ===== ==== ==== ==== ==== ==== ==== ==== ==== =
# Step 1: Set Your API Key
# ===== ==== ==== ==== ==== ==== ==== ==== ==== =
os.environ["OPENAI_API_KEY"] = "your-openai-api-key"


# ===== ==== ==== ==== ==== ==== ==== ==== ==== =
# Step 2: Prepare Your Local Documents
# ===== ==== ==== ==== ==== ==== ==== ==== ==== =
# Ingest and chunk custom documents
raw_text = """
```

Quantum computing uses quantum bits (qubits) that leverage superposition and entanglement.

Post-quantum cryptography is being developed to counter quantum threats to classical encryption.

Major breakthroughs in 2024 include advancements in superconducting qubits and error correction.

***

```python
text_splitter = RecursiveCharacterTextSplitter(chunk_size=300,
chunk_overlap=50)

docs = text_splitter.split_text(raw_text)


# Create embeddings and a local FAISS vector store
embeddings = OpenAIEmbeddings(model="text-embedding-3-small")
vectorstore = FAISS.from_texts(docs, embeddings)


# RAG pipeline for local document retrieval
local_rag = RetrievalQA.from_chain_type(
    llm=ChatOpenAI(model_name="gpt-4", temperature=0),
    retriever=vectorstore.as_retriever(),
    return_source_documents=True
)


# ==== ==== ==== === ==== ==== ==== ==== ==== ====
# Step 3: Add External Tool Integrations
# ==== ==== ==== === ==== ==== ==== ==== ==== ====
# Tool 1: Wikipedia Search
wiki_tool = Tool(
    name="Wikipedia Search",
    func=WikipediaAPIWrapper().run,
    description="Searches Wikipedia for additional facts."
```

```
)


# Tool 2: Local RAG

local_tool = Tool(

    name="Local Knowledge Base",

    func=local_rag.run,

    description="Answers questions based on local documents."

)



# ================================================
# Step 4: Initialize Agentic RAG (ReAct + Tools)
# ================================================

llm = ChatOpenAI(model_name="gpt-4", temperature=0)

agent = initialize_agent(

    tools=[wiki_tool, local_tool],

    llm=llm,

    agent="zero-shot-react-description",

    verbose=True

)



# ================================================
# Step 5: Multi-Hop Query Example
# ================================================

query = "Summarize the latest quantum computing breakthroughs and their impact
on cybersecurity."

response = agent.run(query)



# ================================================
# Step 6: Display Final Answer
```

```
# ==== ==== ===== === ==== ==== ==== ==== ==== ====
```

print("\n--- Final Answer ---")

print(response)

How This Agentic Template Works

1. **Local Knowledge Base:** Uses FAISS with OpenAI embeddings for fast retrieval from custom documents.

2. **Wikipedia Integration:** Queries external sources dynamically when local knowledge is insufficient.

3. **Agentic Reasoning (ReAct):** The agent decides which tool to use, retrieves results, and iteratively plans multi-step actions.

4. **Multi-Hop Retrieval:** Combines data from multiple sources (local docs + Wikipedia) before synthesizing a final answer.

Key Features

- **Multi-Hop Reasoning:** The agent retrieves additional context step-by-step, not in a single pass.

- **Tool-Oriented Design:** Easy to extend with more tools (APIs, SQL queries, calculators).

- **Hybrid Data Use:** Combines internal company data with external web resources.

Next Expansion Ideas

- Add **PDF ingestion** with PyPDFLoader or UnstructuredFileLoader.

- Implement **Agentic RAG loops** with LangGraph for complex multi-step planning.

- Introduce **RAGAS evaluation** for output validation and performance scoring.

- Integrate **vector database services** (e.g., Pinecone or Milvus) for large-scale enterprise data.

Industry-Specific Applications: Tailoring RAG Models for Success

RAG models are not one-size-fits-all. By customizing retrievers, embeddings, and fine-tuning techniques, businesses can achieve domain-specific intelligence across diverse industries. Below are real-world applications and example use cases across healthcare, finance, legal, and e-commerce for 2024–2025.

G.1 Healthcare Applications

RAG can power clinical assistants, research tools, and patient-facing solutions by combining retrieval of medical literature with context-aware generation.

USE CASE	DESCRIPTION	BENEFITS	RAG CUSTOMIZATION
CLINICAL DECISION SUPPORT	Retrieve and synthesize the latest clinical guidelines for specific patient cases.	Improves diagnosis accuracy, reduces medical errors.	Use **BioBERT** embeddings, medical vector databases (PubMed, UMLS).
MEDICAL RESEARCH SUMMARIES	Summarize thousands of medical papers for trends or treatment comparisons.	Saves time for clinicians and researchers.	Multi-hop retrieval with PubMed APIs.
PATIENT-FACING HEALTH BOTS	Provide patients with explanations of lab reports or treatments.	Better patient understanding and engagement.	Instruction-tuned RAG for simplified language.

G.2 Finance Applications

In finance, RAG models are used for risk analysis, portfolio insights, and compliance monitoring.

USE CASE	DESCRIPTION	BENEFITS	RAG CUSTOMIZATION
RISK ASSESSMENT	Retrieve and analyze historical	Enhances risk prediction	Dense retrieval of financial filings and news reports.

	market data and regulatory filings.	and compliance checks.	
PERSONALIZED ADVISORY	Generate real-time investment insights tailored to user portfolios.	Improves financial planning accuracy.	C-RAG with user-specific data filters.
FRAUD DETECTION REPORTS	Summarize suspicious patterns from transaction logs and regulations.	Faster fraud detection and auditing.	Agentic RAG with multi-source retrieval.

G.3 Legal Applications

RAG models streamline legal research, contract review, and case law analysis by retrieving precedents and generating summaries.

USE CASE	DESCRIPTION	BENEFITS	RAG CUSTOMIZATION
CASE LAW RESEARCH	Retrieve relevant precedents and summarize judgments.	Reduces manual research time for legal teams.	Dense RAG with LegalBERT embeddings.
CONTRACT ANALYSIS	Identify clauses, risks, and compliance issues.	Speeds up contract reviews and risk assessment.	Instruction-tuned BART-RAG for structured clause summaries.
COMPLIANCE MONITORING	Scan laws and regulations for updates affecting contracts.	Ensures timely legal compliance.	Hybrid retrieval (keyword + vector search).

G.4 E-Commerce Applications

E-commerce platforms use RAG for personalized recommendations, product Q&A, and dynamic content generation.

USE CASE	DESCRIPTION	BENEFITS	RAG CUSTOMIZATION
PRODUCT SEARCH & Q&A	Retrieve product	Improves user	Dense embeddings for

	descriptions, reviews, and FAQs to answer customer queries.	experience and conversion rates.	semantic product search.
PERSONALIZED RECOMMENDATIONS	Generate recommendations based on user history and trending products.	Increases sales and customer satisfaction.	C-RAG with customer purchase patterns.
DYNAMIC CONTENT GENERATION	Create SEO-friendly product descriptions or blog content.	Saves content generation time and cost.	BART-RAG fine-tuned for e-commerce tone.

G.5 Key Trends Across Industries (2024–2025)

- **Healthcare:** Rise of Agentic RAG for multi-step research on clinical trials and patient records.
- **Finance:** Growing use of real-time vector search + retrieval from live data feeds (SEC filings, stock reports).
- **Legal:** Integration of compliance rule engines with RAG-based assistants for faster legal audits.
- **E-commerce:** AI-driven semantic search and recommendation engines powered by multi-modal RAG (text + images).

Key Takeaway

Tailoring RAG with domain-specific embeddings, fine-tuned decoders, and curated knowledge bases is the key to maximizing its impact across industries.

About the Author

I'm Vijay, with nearly two decades in the tech arena, particularly passionate about demystifying artificial intelligence (AI) to make it accessible and engaging.

AI fascinates me for its transformative potential across various sectors, driving my career towards illuminating its complexities and practical benefits for societal advancement. This book is an extension of that mission, aiming to simplify RAG models a blend of retrieval-based and generative AI systems for a broad audience.

RAG models stand at the forefront of AI innovation, combining information retrieval with generative capabilities to enhance AI's contextual awareness and response accuracy. This book seeks to bridge theoretical AI concepts with real-world applications, catering to both AI enthusiasts and newcomers.

Vijay Bhoyar

Refer More Learnings @

www.aiamigos.org

www.aieducationforkids.com

Vijay Bhoyar

www.ingramcontent.com/pod-product-compliance
Lightning Source LLC
LaVergne TN
LVHW051746050326
832903LV00029B/2747